Original title:
Witty Whispers in the Woods

Copyright © 2025 Creative Arts Management OÜ
All rights reserved.

Author: Charles Whitfield
ISBN HARDBACK: 978-1-80567-454-2
ISBN PAPERBACK: 978-1-80567-753-6

The Mischievous Melody of Mellifluous Monsters

In a glade where giggles bloom,
Monsters dance in playful gloom.
With silly hats and clumsy feet,
They turn the forest into a treat.

One jester swings from a crooked tree,
Tickling leaves with wild glee.
A chorus of croaks, and a quack or two,
Makes the shadows laugh, who knew?

A ticklish breeze wraps 'round the boughs,
With whispers of mischief, we take our vows.
To splash in puddles and race the breeze,
Chasing the sun, as light as we please.

Beneath the starlit, twinkling dome,
Each furry face feels right at home.
They share their tales with laughter bright,
Turning the dark into pure delight.

Spry Serenades of the Shrubland

In the thicket, squirrels prance,
Chasing shadows, in a dance.
Rabbits giggle, tails a-flitter,
As the branches play their critter flitter.

Bushy tales of brave raccoons,
Singing loud beneath the moons.
With every rustle, laughter grows,
Nature's humor, as the breeze blows.

The Jovial Whisper of Wandering Winds

A breeze carries whispers low,
Tickling leaves, watch them blow.
Trees chuckle, shaking their boughs,
Sharing secrets, no one knows.

With every gust, a giggle flies,
Swirling tales beneath bright skies.
Clouds join in, as they float by,
Tickling sunbeams, oh so spry!

Mirthful Murmurs under the Moonlit Mulberry

Underneath the silver glow,
Crickets chirp a lively show.
Fireflies wink, casting light,
As shadows dance, a pure delight.

Jokes exchanged between the vines,
Causing laughter, weaving lines.
The moon, a witness to the fun,
While leafy friends bask in the sun.

The Cheerful Chat of Canopied Companions

In the canopy, voices rise,
Chirping birds, with comical guise.
Squirrels share some nutty jokes,
As branches bounce, while laughter stokes.

From ferny edges, giggles sprout,
In cozy nooks, there's no doubt.
Nature's friends, in harmony,
Crafting joy, wild and free.

Questions from Quaking Quercus

Why do the squirrels wear little hats?
Do they think they're funny? Or just for the chats?
Where do the rabbits learn all their tricks?
Is their school hidden? Or part of the mix?

What if the owls are just night-time jesters?
Telling tall tales with winged investors?
Do the leaves gossip when the wind starts to play?
Or do they keep secrets, just fading away?

Capers of the Courteous Canopy

The branches bow low, a polite little dance,
While the breezes giggle at each leaf's prance.
What if the sun is a shy, blushing orb?
Playing a game with its playful absorb?

High in the boughs are the chattering crows,
With a secret they share that nobody knows.
Do they trade jokes over acorns and snacks?
In this leafy realm, humor never lacks.

The Delightful Dialogue of Dappled Light

In patches of gold, the sunlight will tease,
Chasing shadows around with the greatest of ease.
Do the flowers flirt with the passing breeze?
Or just sway along, like they're under a freeze?

What's that soft chuckle from the moss-covered stones?
Maybe it's laughter from the gnomes and their phones.
Is there a punchline to the tales that they weave?
Or a tickling joke up their textured sleeve?

Rambling Reflections of the Restless Roots

Beneath the earth, what secrets do dwell?
Do roots swap stories, like rings in a shell?
Is the soil a comedian, rich in its jest,
With puns in the dirt and a punchline to test?

As twigs snap and crackle, what's staged in the night?
Do they gather for stories by flickering light?
If trees can chuckle, in their own quiet zest,
Then surely the woods are a jesters' grand fest!

Forest Folly and Fern Frivolity

In the shade where shadows dance,
Flowers giggle at a squirrel's prance.
Mushrooms wear their spotted crowns,
As chattering birds spin silly sounds.

A rabbit hops with such great flair,
Jumps in circles, without a care.
The brook chuckles at a fish's jest,
While the old tree leans back to rest.

Ants in lines, with tiny grins,
Playing tag, they bump and spin.
Even the breeze, with playful tease,
Rearranges leaves with charming ease.

Each corner hides a playful snare,
Where laughter flows in the cool air.
Nature's humor, wild and free,
Whirls around like a giggling spree.

Echoes of Eclectic Enchantment

Hooting owls share silly jokes,
While gnomes giggle behind large oaks.
The stream prattles with glee so bright,
Reflecting sparkles of pure delight.

A dancing frog in a glittery coat,
Croaks a tune, and the crickets emote.
Fireflies twinkle in rhythmic bliss,
Flirting around without a miss.

The wind carries tales of laughter near,
Where treetops shake without fear.
Squirrels debate on the best acorn,
In this land where laughter is born.

Echoes blend in a symphony,
Nature's own light-hearted harmony.
With every twist and turn we take,
Magic sparkles in every wake.

Tales Told by the Twisting Trails

Along the paths where shadows tease,
Dancing footprints sway in the breeze.
The rocks whisper secrets, ages old,
Of playful spirits, brash and bold.

The trails wind like a wiggly worm,
Leading to tales that twist and turn.
Each step whispers a little prank,
A flutter here, a giggle rank.

Every corner, a new surprise,
Enchanted fun beneath bright skies.
Chipmunks race and squirrels cheer,
The forest alive with joy sincere.

As the sun sets in golden hue,
Night invites the laughter too.
With every path that bends away,
The woods are full of a merry play.

The Riddles of Rustling Leaves

Amidst the rustle, secrets hide,
The leaves sigh softly, a nature guide.
With a flap and flutter, they mime a tale,
Of squirrels plotting a daring sail.

Each branch beckons a jesting breeze,
Whisking away with curious ease.
Crickets chirp in cryptic rhyme,
Tickling the air, they keep good time.

Hidden creatures peek with delight,
Sharing giggles under the moonlight.
The forest floor, a game of spies,
Where laughter echoes and never dies.

In every rustle, a riddle's spun,
To tease the mind and have some fun.
So listen close, if you dare believe,
The magic lives in the rustling leaves.

Quips and Quirks in the Thicket

In the thicket where squirrels chat,
They argue over who's the best acrobat.
One swears he can leap over the brook,
While another claims he's quite the cook.

A rabbit giggles, tail all a-fluff,
Says, 'You're all crazy, but that's not enough!'
They wager a carrot on who'll take flight,
As owls snicker softly, enjoying the night.

Lighthearted Lore of the Leafy Realm

A fox dons a hat made of leaves and twine,
Proclaiming he's royalty, feeling divine.
The deer roll their eyes, legs crossed in jest,
Claiming the fox is no more than a pest.

The brook bubbles on, sharing tales with the moss,
'Who's the best dancer?' it splashes across.
A frog hops in, all jazz with a leap,
"I'll teach you to jig, let's revel and peep!"

Tales Told Underneath Twinkling Stars

Under the stars where the crickets croon,
The raccoons argue, their plans all a-boon.
One wants a feast, the other a ball,
But ends up just stealing from crates in the hall.

A badger dressed fancy, with sequins galore,
Protests, "Let's dance, not forage for more!"
They sway in the shadows, a comical sight,
With laughter that echoes and fills up the night.

Whimsical Revelations at Woodland Crossroads

At crossroads of paths where the shadows play,
A hedgehog debates if he'll go or stay.
"Left or right, which leads to the fun?
Maybe both, we'll see when the day is done!"

A wise old owl hoots, "Just follow the breeze,
But be cautious of squirrels, they'll steal with ease!"
The hedgehog chuckles, "What's life without a jest?
Let's all have a laugh, it's surely the best!"

Hidden Jests among the Pines

A squirrel in a top hat,
Dancing on a twig,
Pinecones start to roll,
As laughter starts to dig.

The raccoon wears a mask,
Pretends to be a thief,
Stealing acorns for fun,
In search of comic relief.

The owls exchange a glance,
With a wink that says it all,
While the rabbits play charades,
At the base of the tall wall.

In the shade of the boughs,
Giggles fill the air,
Nature's own comedians,
Who live without a care.

Chortles of the Canopy

Up high in the branches,
A parrot tells a joke,
The trees sway and chuckle,
As laughter starts to poke.

A frog leaping for flies,
Gets tangled in a vine,
With each failed attempt,
He croaks, 'This should be fine!'

Bees buzzing with glee,
Share gossip in the hive,
'Have you heard about the fox?'
'He thinks he can't be dived!'

The leaves dance with mirth,
In a rustling brigade,
Nature's sense of humor,
In every glade displayed.

Secrets of the Sprightly Shrubs

Underneath the bushes,
A hedgehog spins a tale,
Of a snail who ran fast,
And a tortoise who'd wail.

With a wink to the ferns,
He rolls over with glee,
'Who knew my jokes were so good,
They'd sprout from each tree?'

A hedgerow full of giggles,
Nestles the clever gnome,
Peeking out from his door,
He'll never leave his home.

With a quip and a laugh,
Every shrub comes alive,
To jest with one another,
In secret they contrive!

Laughter Lurking in Leafy Shadows

Amid the dappled light,
A badger snickers low,
At the lines of silly haikus,
That the fox just wrote for show.

The trees lean in closer,
To catch the sly remarks,
As the chipmunks play tag,
Leaving their funny sparks.

A dance of shadows twist,
As the sunlight plays tricks,
While the moths make mischief,
With their flickering flicks.

In the forest, giggles echo,
Through the branches above,
In a realm of pure laughter,
Nature's joy weaves like a glove.

Shenanigans of the Swaying Saplings

Tiny trunks with lots to say,
Dancing leaves in a playful sway.
They giggle as the breezes tease,
Whispering jokes among the trees.

Squirrels laugh, they join the fun,
Tumbling down in morning sun.
With acorn hats and cheeky glee,
They pull pranks beneath each tree.

Lively tales in every rustle,
A hidden punchline makes them hustle.
Branches stretch to catch the light,
Sharing secrets till the night.

In this grove, the spirits play,
Turning moments bright and gay.
Every bark a laugh, a jest,
In nature's court, they are the best.

Smarty-Pants Secrets of the Spruces

Tall and proud, the spruces stand,
Holding knowledge, quite well planned.
With needles sharp, they point and poke,
Every breeze a clever joke.

They've seen the tales of passing deer,
And every chuckle one can hear.
The owls nod as if to say,
'It's laugh-a-minute every day!'

In the moonlight, shadows dance,
Spruces share their secret chance.
With every sway and subtle shift,
They pass along a clever gift.

Roots that twist in laughter's grip,
With every gust, they start to zip.
Smarty-pants without a doubt,
In their forest, giggles sprout.

Roaming Riddles in the Rustling Grass

Through the blades, the breezes swirl,
Riddles jump and twirl and whirl.
Grasshoppers giggle with delight,
Bouncing in a sunny fight.

Each blade carries tales anew,
Tickling toes, as you pass through.
Caterpillars in fine dress,
Challenge friends to guess and guess.

In the shade, the shadows blend,
Whispers fly from end to end.
Nature's puzzles, bright and bold,
With every riddle, laughter unfolds.

A tickling breeze that won't relent,
Brings joy and jest, with no lament.
In this patch of green and gold,
Funny stories will be told.

The Charming Chuckles of the Canopied Realm

In leafy homes where sunlight streams,
Charming chuckles weave through dreams.
Birds chirp jokes from up so high,
While squirrels grin as they pass by.

Underneath the canopy's shade,
Whimsical stories are lovingly laid.
Each rustle brings a laugh or two,
In the realm of green, all is true.

Beneath the branches, playful sights,
Friends gather for their giggling nights.
With every word, a hearty cheer,
In the forest, there's nothing to fear.

So come along, let laughter reign,
In every leaf, there's joy to gain.
For in this realm where charms prevail,
Every chuckle tells the tale.

Secrets Under the Starry Canopy

Beneath the stars, the critters scheme,
A raccoon dons a moonlit dream.
The owl nudges with a playful stare,
And whispers tales of midnight flair.

Squirrels giggle from lofty heights,
Dreaming up their snack-filled nights.
Chipmunks prank the sleepy deer,
Each hidden laugh floats sweet and clear.

The fireflies flicker, dance in glee,
Painting stories for all to see.
While shadows chuckle with delight,
In this forest of pure midnight light.

This night of fun will surely end,
But these tales will twist and bend.
Tomorrow's dawn, a brand new page,
With secrets to share, we'll engage.

Silly Secrets of the Sycamore Scene

Up in the sycamore, squirrels play,
Telling jokes to pass the day.
A nutty riddle, a peppy pun,
They laugh in chorus, oh what fun!

The branches sway with a rhythmic cheer,
As birds chirp freely, loud and clear.
Nestled close, a fox peers in,
Joining the laughter with a cheeky grin.

The wind tosses leaves like silly hats,
As the rabbits gather, scattered chats.
A ponderous turtle joins the fray,
And suddenly, it's all a relay!

When twilight softens every sound,
The whispers hold, of giggles abound.
In this nook of nature's cheer,
A sweet slice of joy, we hold dear.

Quirky Quotes from the Curious Creek

By the winding creek where laughter flows,
A frog recites what no one knows.
'Life is but a hop and skip!'
He croaks, then takes a big green dip.

Nearby, a hedgehog sprinkles sass,
With prickly wisdom from the grass.
'If you can laugh, then you're alright!'
He snorts, then rolls beneath the light.

The fish below flip funny fins,
While crickets chirp their tiny sins.
Echoes bounce from stone to stone,
Charming secrets, keenly known.

As dusk draws near, the chatter blends,
With giggles shared among good friends.
In the twist and curl of nature's rhyme,
Jokes linger sweetly, transcending time.

Lively Laments of the Leafy Library

In the leafy library, pages rustle,
A wise old owl gives a gentle shuffle.
'Why did the tree join the band?'
With a wink, he waves his feathered hand.

A rabbit hops to check out a tale,
While mice put on a playful veil.
'It's the roots of joy that matter most,'
They giggle softly like a friendly ghost.

The branches sway to the whispered lore,
As laughter echoes forevermore.
A tale of tricks, of mischief bright,
Under boughs that twinkle with delight.

And when the sun bids night goodbye,
Their giddiness fills the twilight sky.
Books tucked tight, laughter stays,
In this library where fun always plays.

Playful Patters on the Pine Needles

Breezes dance with leaves so bright,
Squirrels scamper, what a sight!
A chipmunk jokes, with cheeks so wide,
As shadows play, the fun can't hide.

Mossy floors, where laughter grows,
A playful pup, with toes like bows.
The sunbeams wink, as if they know,
What mischief hides in green below.

Frogs crack jokes by the pond's soft edge,
While turtles ponder life's great pledge.
A butterfly flits with a cheeky beat,
In this green realm, where mirth's a treat.

The Hidden Humor in Harmony's Haven

In a glen where giggles swell,
A rabbit tales, it spins so well.
With carrot crowns and fluffy tails,
It tipsy-tops along the trails.

Birds belt tunes with clucky cheer,
Foxes laugh, but not too near.
They know the game, the forest's jest,
In shadows where the sunlight rests.

Whispers flutter from tree to tree,
As ants parade, a conga spree.
Mushrooms chuckle, it's quite the show,
Nature's circus, come see below!

Breezy Buffoonery Among the Bare Branches

Crickets chirp in funny tones,
As hedgehogs roll, they save their bones.
A windy whim calls out to all,
Inviting every beast, great and small.

The wind weaves tales in rustling leaves,
Where buzzing bees create mischief heaves.
A wise old owl, who's hard to outsmart,
Plays tricks on the dawn, as day's about to start.

Breezes tease the would-be wise,
Twirling dandelions as they rise.
Each bare branch holds a secret prank,
Where sights and sounds dance down the bank.

Giggles in the Glimmering Glade

In a glade where sparkles gleam,
Laughter flows like a babbling stream.
Fireflies waltz in a dazzling line,
While moonbeams giggle and brightly shine.

Bouncing bunnies hop with glee,
Underneath the old oak tree.
A raccoon plays with shadows cast,
In this joyful world, time flies fast.

The night is alive with a ticklish tease,
As constellations wink, with gentle ease.
Here in the magic where whims abound,
Every twinkling star joins the sound.

Clever Conversations in the Canopy

High above the ground they chatter,
Leaves with laughter, oh what a clatter.
Squirrels gossip, birds exchange glee,
In a swaying dance, so wild and free.

Raccoons debate on nutty delights,
A wise old owl joins the witty flights.
Branches above hold secrets tight,
In the treetops, everything feels right.

A hare hops by on a curious quest,
Eavesdropping on banter, never a rest.
The sun peeks through with a teasing grin,
In such a place, the fun begins.

Twigs snap underfoot, a playful sound,
Nature's comedy, all around.
Whispers of joy, in the breeze they fly,
In this lively realm, let laughter cry.

Murmurs of Mischief in the Meadow

In the field where daisies bloom,
Critters gather to escape their gloom.
Bunnies jest with gardening glee,
While butterflies join in, wild and free.

A cheeky fox tells tales so grand,
Of trickster antics across the land.
Grasshoppers giggle, their tunes bright,
In the meadow, everything feels right.

The wind carries tales of silly show,
Of past pranks and where they did go.
With every rustle, a chuckle rings,
Nature together, the fun it brings.

At dusk they settle, the stars come out,
Whispers of mischief fill the route.
In the meadow's heart, so light and gay,
Happiness rests as night claims the day.

Enchanted Echoes within the Emerald Grove

Deep in the grove, where shadows dance,
Light shimmering down, a playful glance.
Mice share secrets in rhythmic bursts,
While insects chirp with comical quirks.

A tree stump holds a council of sorts,
Where wise woodpeckers share their retorts.
Laughter echoes through the dense trees,
In this enchanted realm, all is at ease.

The breeze grabs whispers from every side,
Twisting them into a giggling tide.
Vines intertwine, as if to embrace,
Each funny tale finds its perfect place.

When twilight falls, a party ignites,
Frogs croak rhythms, in joyous flights.
All creatures join, beneath leafy shrouds,
In their green paradise, laughter loud.

Jests and Jingles among the Tree Trunks

Among the trunks where shadows play,
Little creatures find time to sway.
A squirrel spins tales of daring feats,
While chipmunks dance to fun, quick beats.

The trees hold court in a rustic space,
Where laughter echoes, a warm embrace.
Every bark tells a story so true,
Of adventures taken and mischief anew.

A breeze carries a sound, blending cheer,
Tickling leaves as they rustle near.
Foxes roll on the forest floor,
Playing their tricks, always wanting more.

As night unfolds under starry skies,
The constellations spark with guiding eyes.
Jests and jingles fill every nook,
In the heart of the woods, magic's book.

Giggling Glimpses of the Great Outdoors

In the thicket, squirrels play,
Chasing shadows throughout the day.
A rabbit hops with a cheeky grin,
While the wise old owl twirls a win.

The trees are filled with chitter and chatter,
"Who's the fastest?" they question, a matter.
A fox shows off with a little dance,
While butterflies join in a swirling prance.

The brook sings sweetly, a snicker here,
Frogs croak jokes that you can overhear.
The sun peeks through with a playful beam,
Nature hums tunes like a silly dream.

As twilight falls, the crickets kick in,
Their song a riddle, a playful spin.
The stars twinkle with a giggle divine,
Nature's charm is simply, oh-so-fine.

Nature's Nifty Nook of Nonsense

Beneath the leaves, a secret chat,
A chipmunk claiming he's quite the cat.
"Did you see that chase, oh what a sight!"
His friends all laugh, filled with delight.

The flowers giggle as breezes tease,
Ticklish petals dance with ease.
A snail takes selfies, slow but bold,
Capturing stories of adventures untold.

The ants march in a disciplined line,
But trip on twigs—oh, what a sign!
"Next time wear shoes, your feet will thank!"
With tiny toots, they share their prank.

As dusk rolls in, the fun won't cease,
The fireflies wink, spreading their peace.
In this nook, laughter knows no bounds,
In nature's jest, joy knows no grounds.

Bubbles of Banter in the Breezy Boughs

Up high aflight, the birds convene,
With feathers bright and voices keen.
"Who can sing the highest note?"
They chirp and chatter in a merry quote.

The branches sway, a laughing spree,
A whole crew of squirrels in jubilee.
"Race you to that acorn, quick!"
Their tiny feet patter, all so slick.

A breeze whistles through the leafy lane,
Carrying giggles, a sweet refrain.
"Did you hear the one about the bee?"
Buzzing with humor, wild and free.

As dusk spreads joy on a golden stage,
Creatures gather, ready to engage.
In the heart of nature, friendship swells,
With bubbles of banter, their laughter dwells.

Jestful Journeys into the Green Abyss

Through tangled trails, the path is sly,
Where mushrooms grumble as we pass by.
"Why so glum?" a fern does tease,
"Shake off that wood dirt, let's have ease!"

The critters convene for a comedy show,
A hedgehog's punchline steals the glow.
"Why don't we ever tell secrets to trees?"
"Because they always bark, oh please!"

Down by the pond, frogs leap in style,
Their jumps like jokes, creating a smile.
"Did you hear the one about the fish?"
"Let's reel in laughter, it's quite delish!"

As night cloaks all in a velvet hue,
Stars join in with laughter, pure and true.
In this abyss, joy never ends,
For nature's jest is where laughter blends.

The Mischief of Moonlit Foliage

Under the silver beam, trees sway,
Squirrel spies a shadow play.
With a leap and a bound, oh what a sight,
Frogs in tuxedos dance through the night.

Breezes flutter, laughter comes alive,
Owls hoot jokes that make us thrive.
In the neon glow of the mushrooms' dance,
Even the grumpiest raccoon takes a chance.

Fireflies twinkle, flickering bright,
Crickets play melodies, all feel light.
A hedgehog in a bow tie struts by,
While butterflies giggle and happily fly.

With every rustle, a tale unfolds,
Of secret gatherings never told.
Nature's jesters, a riotous crew,
Leave us with smiles, pure and true.

Antics of the Enchanted Glade

Beneath a bough, a rabbit schemes,
Drawing plans of wildest dreams.
A fox in a cape throws leaves in the air,
While mushrooms giggle without a care.

The turtles play poker, I swear it's true,
With acorns as chips, their fortunes accrue.
Squirrels trade secrets, whispers so sly,
As butterflies flutter and wave goodbye.

Sunbeams giggle through branches above,
Painting the scene with endless love.
The breeze carries jokes from the bumblebee,
Creating a buzz that sets us free.

In this merry glade where mischief thrives,
Every creature knows how to jive.
From the tiny ants with their marching tune,
To the merry-go-round of the playful raccoon.

Giggles among the Gnarled Roots

Tangled roots hide laughter so bold,
Where stories of silliness dare to unfold.
Tree trunks chuckle with wisdom to share,
As fawns play peekaboo, unaware.

Mice host tea parties with oversized hats,
While hedgehogs slide down like acrobat rats.
In the depths of the thicket, all join the spree,
Nature's grand circus is ongoing, you see!

Jays squawk jokes that tickle the ear,
While fireflies twirl, spreading good cheer.
A raccoon wears shades, looking quite fab,
Sipping dew tea from a littlest lab.

With roots that twist and vines that dance,
Every corner invites a chance.
To let out a laugh, to have some fun,
Among the gnarled roots, the games are never done.

A Howl of Humor in the Hollow

Deep in the hollow where shadows creep,
A wolf tells tales that make you leap.
Caught in his charm, the night turns bright,
As giggles echo with sheer delight.

Foxes join in with their clever quips,
Sharing whispers with playful flips.
Bats chuckle softly as they swoop low,
Creating a scene of delightful row.

Raccoons on stilts, don't fall, I plea,
The moonlight glistens, as we all agree.
With orange pumpkins rolling like balls,
Laughter rings out, as the evening calls.

The stars join the fun in this playful show,
Casting their wink on the woodland glow.
Cranes crack wise with a tap of their feet,
In this hollow, humor and harmony meet.

Forest Fables and Playful Patter

In the forest where secrets crawl,
Squirrels gossip, having a ball.
With tiny paws, they crack a jest,
While the wise old owl just takes rest.

Beneath the trees, shadows play,
Bees hum tunes, hip-hip-hip-hooray.
A fox in a hat struts with flair,
While rabbits giggle without a care.

Frogs leap in sync to a tune,
Hopping along with a dance so maroon.
Their croaking notes blend in the air,
Creating a melody, funny and rare.

With laughter stitched in the leaves above,
Every creature shares its love.
In this grove, joy grabs the stage,
As nature writes its own funny page.

Banter Beneath the Bark

A woodpecker pecks with a rhythm divine,
Chasing the echoes of jokes in line.
A raccoon winks with a sly little grin,
As squirrels debate who will win.

"Why did the tree refuse to talk?"
Asked a hedgehog on his daily walk.
"Because it would leaf you in tears!"
They all burst out laughing, quelled their fears.

The sun spills laughter through boughs so wide,
While beetles march with a jolly stride.
A chummy old badger, wise and spry,
Joins in the fun with a twinkling eye.

The banter flows like a bubbly stream,
In this woodland of mirth, life's a dream.
Under the bark, where stories are spun,
Nature's humor is never done.

The Sprightly Soundtrack of the Glade

Hoots and howls compose a song,
In the glade where all creatures belong.
Crickets chirp a tune so bright,
While foxes twirl in the moonlight.

A porcupine wearing tiny shades,
Sways in rhythm, dancing in parades.
The laughter echoes, round and round,
With a melody that joyfully resounds.

Twig percussion and leafy strings,
Nature's band plays all sorts of things.
Bees beatbox, with bumbles and hums,
As playful pranks and good times come.

Each note dances on the breeze,
Inviting all to join with ease.
This cheerful soundscape, wild and free,
Is a melody of pure glee.

Chortles and Chirps of the Woodland Creatures

Chirps and chortles fill the air,
Amidst the trees, without a care.
A giggling chipmunk tells a tale,
While clumsy deer trip on a trail.

"Who left the acorns on the ground?"
Grumbled a rabbit, turning around.
The wise old turtle had a thought,
"This forest plays more tricks than sought!"

The frogs invite friends to jump in,
While buzzing bees spin tales of sin.
A dance-off starts, feet all a-twirl,
As the woodland spins in a crazy whirl.

Through the branches, laughter weaves,
From playful hearts, humor achieves.
In this animated, merry retreat,
Nature's creatures share a funny beat.

Puckish Parables in the Pinewood Path

In a patch of sunlight, shadows dance,
Squirrels exchange secretive glances.
A rabbit poses like a highbrow sage,
While a turtle writes jokes on a leafy page.

Underneath the tall, swaying trees,
A crow cracks puns, bringing the bees.
Chirps of laughter float through the air,
As the wise old owl gives a cheeky stare.

A fox tells tales of the cleverest hare,
Each story spun leaves the forest bare.
Tales of pranks with a wink and a nod,
Nature's humor—timeless and odd.

With giggles and snickers, the night descends,
Even moss has a chuckle, as daylight ends.
The brook bubbles softly, sharing its jest,
In this merry woodland, laughter's a quest.

The Capering Cider of the Cedar Grove

Among the cedars, a party unfolds,
With cider that sparkles and stories retold.
The fawns prance about, their hooves find the beat,
While raccoons serve snacks, oh what a treat!

A gopher in glasses gives a grand toast,
To the critters who dance, he highlights the most.
With swirls and twirls, they twine in the spray,
A beaver beats drums, leading the fray.

The laughter erupts like the bubbles in stew,
Every critter joins in, oh, what a view!
A badger does splits on a log, quite the show,
While hedgehogs hum tunes as they steal the show.

As the moon climbs high, with stars all aglow,
The cider keeps flowing, this party won't slow.
In the grove where trees sway, and silliness thrives,
These playful spirits ensure joy survives.

Flirtations of the Forest Floor

On the forest floor, where shadows play coy,
A pair of chipmunks enjoy a sweet ploy.
With tiny flirtations and winks in between,
Their antics spill laughter, a charming scene.

The ladybugs twirl, wearing spots like a crown,
While beetles perform a soft, bouncy gown.
Each flower joins in with a colorful sigh,
As the breeze carries whispers of flirty goodbye.

A snail, rather slow, tries to woo with a note,
Dancing on petals, his heart's full of hope.
Each pause is a chance for their eyes to meet,
Nature's rom-com with a humorous beat.

Underneath the moon's watchful, gleaming eye,
The forest holds secrets of love's cheeky lie.
In this playful domain, connections do thrive,
Where creatures find joy in feeling alive.

Cheery Chirps and Cheeky Chatter

Amidst the branches, a chorus takes flight,
Birds gossip and cackle, delighting the night.
A parrot misquotes with a twisty charm,
While the magpie crafts tales that raise alarm.

Gregarious squirrels swap the juiciest news,
As butterflies flutter, sporting bright hues.
Each chirp is a chuckle, a gentle tease,
In the canopy high, laughter drifts with ease.

A turtle winks at a snail, quite perplexed,
"Life's a race," he muses, "but I'm quite relaxed."
The trees sway and listen, wearing a grin,
For every sly comment, there's laughter within.

With stars twinkling brightly, the night comes alive,
In this lively nook where the jests never dive.
Cheerful banter flows like a sweet, teasing song,
In the heart of the woods, where they all belong.

Amusing Anecdotes from the Underbrush

A squirrel in a bowtie, so neat,
Flips acorns like a boss, quite a feat.
Tells tales of his travels on a breeze,
While birds chuckle softly in the trees.

A rabbit with a top hat and cane,
Swears he can hop faster than a train.
But as he jumps, he trips on a root,
And giggles erupt from his fuzzy boot.

A raccoon in glasses reads a book,
On how to avoid a nearby cook.
He nods in wisdom, eyes all aglow,
'Just stay away from the barbecue show!'

The fireflies dance, all agog at the show,
As critters swap stories, giggles do grow.
In the underbrush where the laughter is free,
Nature's own jesters, as jolly as can be.

Jestful Journeys through the Timber

A bear with a backpack goes on a hike,
His snack left behind, oh what a strike!
He grumbles and tumbles, 'Where's my pie?'
While a fox giggles near, oh me, oh my!

A hedgehog on roller-skates speeds past,
Bellowing jokes, his humor steadfast.
He spins and he twirls, a sight to behold,
With quills flying about, never too bold.

An owl on a pole gives advice every night,
'Wise up,' he hoots, 'not every flight's right!'
The animals laugh, they chuckle with glee,
As wisdom and wit blend in harmony.

Together they wander, laughter the key,
In their lively journeys, wild and carefree.
Through timber and trails, the joy never shies,
As nature's own jesters share jokes under skies.

Snickers in the Sylvan Sanctuary

A moose with a mustache, quite the sight,
Tells tales of his glory, a woodland knight.
He claims he once danced with a lovely deer,
While everyone snickers, it's loud and clear.

A chipmunk with maracas shakes to the beat,
As he leads a parade down the forest street.
With each little jig, laughter fills the air,
Leaving everyone grinning, without a care.

The trees sway and giggle, whispering lore,
Of all the shenanigans that happened before.
In the sanctuary where hilarity flows,
Nature's own comedy, everyone knows.

Underneath the stars where the shadows play,
Silly stories mingle till the break of day.
With snickers and chuckles floating so high,
A celebration of joy beneath the night sky.

Revelry of the Ravine

In a ravine, a party begins every night,
With critters in crowns, oh, what a sight!
Bats do the limbo, and frogs keep the score,
While the raccoons dance, begging for more.

A porcupine chef, with his special stew,
Claims it'll make you laugh, it's utterly true.
But one forkful later, with a comedic pause,
Everyone erupts—he forgot the sauce!

They gather around, under the moon's glow,
Telling tall tales of the times they say, 'Whoa!'
From the hedgehog who sang to the wise old tree,
Every tale spins laughter, wild and free.

As the night wears on, they toast with delight,
To the joy of their friendship, a beautiful sight.
In the revelry of the ravine, hearts twine,
Laughter and fun, oh, how they shine.

Tales of the Tenacious Thorns

In a garden where roses tease,
A thorn laughed loud, seeking to please.
'Take my advice,' it prickled with glee,
'Life's sharper when you're free as a bee!'

The daisies giggled, rolling their heads,
As the thorns spun tales of daring dreads.
A dandelion said with a puff of cheer,
'At least I'm not stuck with this prickly sphere!'

But one brave thorn had a clever task,
'If you see a bear, just cover your mask!'
The flowers all guffawed, petals flared bright,
While the thorn, oh so bold, just stayed out of sight.

So here lies the jest of the thorny brigade,
Their laughter a shield from the sharpest crusade.
In humor they blossom, a colorful crew,
With tales of thorns that are always true!

Nonsense North of the Nettle

In the grove where the nettles recline,
A squirrel wore spectacles, quite divine.
He juggled acorns with a flourish of flair,
'Watch closely now, if you dare to compare!'

A snail joined in, with a shell on his back,
'Your tricks are so fast, but I'm on the track!'
While laughter erupted from branches up high,
As wise old owls hooted, 'Oh me, oh my!'

The fox told a riddle that tangled their brains,
'What comes without shoes, yet runs in the rains?'
They pondered and pondered, then laughter ensued,
'It's simply a puddle left out to be rude!'

So round and around like a merry-go-round,
The nonsense kept spinning, lost then found.
In the heart of the wild, where humor won't stop,
A party of critters danced till they dropped!

Sprightly Exchanges in Mossy Meadows

In meadows of green where the moss gently grows,
A rabbit in sneakers danced on his toes.
He challenged a hedgehog to race through the fields,
'But remember dear friend, it's my speed that shields!'

The hedgehog just chuckled, with spikes standing tall,
'It's not just about speed, it's the wit after all!'
So they ran side by side, both friends in a whirl,
As butterflies giggled, a fanciful twirl.

Across blooming daisies, they leapt and they pranced,
With each little stumble, the others just danced.
The riddle of time played a game with a wink,
'They're faster than lightning, or perhaps just a blink!'

In this realm of cheer, where each laugh was a gift,
Sprightly exchanges gave every heart a lift.
Mossy meadows echoed, their joy in the air,
With critters united, a whimsical fair!

The Art of Amused Acorns

Among the old oaks, where acorns collide,
A gathering sparked up, oh what a wild ride!
With tales of the forest, both funny and sly,
They cracked up like shells, while the critters flew by.

One acorn stood tall, with a cap made of gold,
'The secret to laughter is daring and bold!'
Then came the wise nut with stories to share,
'Just remember, dear friends, to always beware!'

For squirrels with mischief know how to play,
While raccoons at night steal the show every day.
The laughter was ripe, like an apple in fall,
Echoing through branches, bringing joy to them all.

So gather, dear nuts, for the art of delight,
As joy springs like sap through the warm summer night.
With every small chuckle, let friendship unfold,
In a world full of acorns, each moment's pure gold!

Humorous Hums of the Hedge Witch

In shadows thick, the broomstick flies,
The hedge witch cackles, her laughter defies.
With potions brewed from odd vegetable,
She claims to cure all, not just a few credible.

An owl hoots loud, with a sarcastic grin,
'You call that a spell? Let the chaos begin!'
Her plants all giggle, the toadstools spin,
In a world of nonsense, the fun's about to begin.

Sprightly fairies dance with delight,
Chasing their shadows in the pale moonlight.
A raccoon in shades joins the merry parade,
His jokes make the mushrooms burst into a cascade.

When the night falls quiet and the stars shine bright,
The hedge witch winks, her heart full of light.
For in her domain, the silly reigns supreme,
With chuckles and charms, it's a whimsical dream.

Enigmatic Echos of the Elms

The elms stand tall, with secrets to share,
Their leaves rustle gossip, through cool evening air.
'Trouble with the squirrels?' whispers a bough,
'Just ask the old owl, he'll tell you how.'

A fox with a smirk claims he's lost his map,
While a chipmunk declares it's a grand old trap.
Echoes of laughter bounce back from the bark,
Where the wise old trees hold their jokes in the dark.

Moonlight spills laughter on glistening dew,
The shadows play games, inventing something new.
With branches that sway, they tease the night breeze,
Sharing tall tales, rope swings, and trees.

In the hollow of trunks, the mischief unfolds,
Each whispering echo, a story retold.
Who knew that the woods had such humor to spare?
In the twilight's embrace, it's the laughter that's rare.

Sassy Stories among the Sturdy Pines

Amongst sturdy pines, a ruckus is heard,
A squirrel spins tales, his dialogue absurd.
'What's that you say? You've seen a big cat?'
A pine cone giggles, 'He's wearing a hat!'

With twirl and a flip, the woodland folks jest,
While the brook hiccups, failing to rest.
The bunny hops near, with an attitude bold,
'In my patch of clover, I'm king to behold!'

A raccoon stands proud, in a mask like a pro,
Claiming to be the local show.
'Tho' the show's not great, the snacks are divine,
Join us in feasting, it's nothing but fine!'

From the dusk till the dawn, their laughter takes flight,
In a realm of sass, everything feels right.
Under the tall pines, no worries to find,
Just playful banter, fun stories entwined.

Playful Parables in the Palisades

In the palisades where the sunlight bends,
Frolicking critters sing songs to their friends.
A badger with charm has a riddle to share,
'What's fluffy and bright and hides in your hair?'

A raccoon in slippers rolls into the scene,
With popcorn delight and a grin so keen.
'Take a wild guess, it's not what you think,
It's all of our joys mixed in with a wink!'

Beneath the tall trees, stories collide,
Each tale more ridiculous, no need to hide.
They laugh at the shadows, play tag with the light,
Taking turns in delight, deep into the night.

As stars twinkle down on the cast so bizarre,
These playful parables reach the moon and star.
Filled with mischief and a pinch of cheer,
In the palisades' heart, laughter draws near.

Whimsical Encounters on Woodland Walks

In the forest, where the squirrels play,
Laughter echoes, brightening the day.
A fox cracks jokes, his tail a twirl,
While rabbits giggle in a frolic swirl.

A raccoon with a mask, so sly and neat,
Tells tall tales while dancing on his feet.
The trees lean close, to catch the sound,
Of silliness blooming all around.

Old owls exchange knowing, wise old winks,
As fungi chuckle, or so it seems.
A deer in a tutu prances with flair,
Creating laughter that fills the air.

So if you wander through these green lanes,
Expect surprises, and silly refrains.
For in the woodlands, where wonders unfold,
Life's all about humor, bright and bold.

The Ha-Ha of the Hidden Thicket.

In thickets dense, where pranks are spun,
A hedgehog jokes, "I'm the prickly one!"
The bushes rustle with secrets and fun,
While the sun peeks in, casting shadows on run.

A turtle tells tales, with pace oh-so-slow,
Of a game of tag with a lightning-quick crow.
With every snicker, the leaves shake and sway,
As laughter bubbles up, come join the play!

Mice with tiny hats hold a tea so grand,
Pour dreams in cups with a steady hand.
A whispered jest from a nearby hare,
Brings fits of giggles to fill the air.

In this thicket, joy's the binding thread,
Where every corner is a joke well said.
So trek through the maze, let smiles ignite,
For hilarity thrives in this woodsy light.

Secret Serenades among the Sylvan Shadows

Beneath the boughs where the shadows dance,
A squirrel sings, giving life a chance.
The grasshoppers join with a phonetic cheer,
Creating melodies only for ears dear.

A bear in a bowtie, all dressed up to toast,
Shares slaps on the back, as he tells ghostly boasts.
While crickets compose, in their rhythmic spree,
Laughter rings out in perfect harmony.

The wind whispers secrets of mischievous ways,
As fireflies glow, lighting up the displays.
And every leaf giggles, a tickled surprise,
As the sun dips low, painting candy-coated skies.

So dance in the shadows, sway with delight,
Where laughter abounds, and everything's right.
In these secret serenades, humor will flow,
In sylvan retreat, let the laughter grow.

Laughter Lurking Beneath Leafy Canopies

Beneath leafy hats where giggles hide,
A bunny hops by with a cheeky stride.
The shadows chuckle at silly pranks,
While nature rejoices in playful ranks.

A raccoon's grin glows under the moon,
He juggles acorns with a comical tune.
With every drop, there's a burst of cheer,
As the forest erupts in a round of dear.

The owls hoot jokes that are witty and sly,
While the fireflies blink as they flutter by.
Leaves rustle softly, a whispering tease,
As laughter takes root in the heart of the trees.

So if you stroll through this canopy bright,
Join the laughter, let your heart take flight.
In hidden corners where the fun spins free,
Nature's humor thrives, as wild as can be.

Playful Echoes in Pine-Scented Air

Squirrels chatter in a sprightly dance,
They argue over acorns, not by chance.
A deer snickers, peeking from behind,
While a raccoon laughs, oh what a find!

Mice wear shoes made of soft tree bark,
Their tiny feet race, leaving a mark.
Bouncing badgers join the fun with glee,
Nature's jesters, wild and free!

The wind tells jokes in a breezy tone,
As pine trees sway, they nod and moan.
The moon chimes in with a silver grin,
While frogs croak rhymes, let the laughs begin!

Under the stars, the laughter grows,
With every rustle, a new tale flows.
In this fragrant world, lighthearted cheer,
Plays in the air, bringing joy near!

Nonsense at the Woodland's Edge

A pancake flipped by a fairy's hand,
Rolling down, it's quite unplanned.
A fox in socks steals all the pies,
As owls quirk up their big, round eyes!

The toadstools dance in polka dots bright,
While shadows waltz with mischievous light.
Come check the antics on this green space,
Where every creature wears a funny face!

The grasses giggle, a ticklish sight,
Telling tales of a llama in flight.
With butterflies trading secrets so sly,
And daisies bowing as the bees fly by!

Silly squirrels wear hats, all askew,
Discussing ripe fruit that's fit to chew.
In this funny land, with mirth as the pledge,
You'll find wild laughter at the woodland's edge!

Whims of the Wildflowers

In the glade where daisies giggle loud,
A tulip twirls, feeling quite proud.
The sun's warm rays toast the humor in bloom,
As petals dance, dispelling all gloom!

Pansies poke fun at the shy little thyme,
While buttercups ballad, keeping in rhyme.
A clover winks with a cheeky smile,
Inviting all friends to stay for a while!

In this jolly patch, where colors collide,
Flowers share puns with joyful pride.
Even the thorns wear a jesting pout,
Embellishing tales that wander about!

With bumblebees buzzing a quirky tune,
The wildflowers laugh 'neath the sun and moon.
Each petal a punchline, a story unfurled,
Creating a laughter-filled, vibrant world!

Frolicsome Fables of the Forest Floor

Nestled low, where sunlight creeps,
Fables of fun in the forest leaps.
A sleepy log disguises a troll,
Who tickles your toes with a jocular goal!

Mushrooms gossip, their caps all aflame,
"I hide the best snacks, it's never the same!"
And tree roots giggle as they intertwine,
Sharing stories of creatures so divine!

Chipmunks bicker, "You stole my nut!"
While a cheeky crow plays the game of strut.
The wind carries laughter, a playful breeze,
Entwining the whispers of the leaves on the trees!

In this merry place, joy knows no bound,
With every step, new chuckles found.
So come and join this frolicsome lore,
Where the forest's heart beats with fun evermore!

The Frothy Frolic of Forest Friends

In a glade where the giggles bloom,
Squirrels swing like acrobats in costume.
Chasing shadows, a dance in delight,
A rabbit trips, oh what a sight!

The frogs croak jokes upon their lily pads,
While owls hoot puns that make us glad.
A deer prances with elegance and flair,
As mischievous winds toss its golden hair.

Beneath a canopy of chatting trees,
The breeze carries laughter, soft as a tease.
Fireflies wink, like stars in disguise,
In this merry realm where nobody cries.

Sunset paints a canvas of cheer,
Adventures await as night draws near.
Friends on a quest, let the fun begin,
In the frothy frolic where joy wears a grin.

Snickers and Secrets in the Underbrush

Amid the ferns where secrets entwine,
A squirrel shares tales, oh so divine.
With a wink and a twitch, he starts to jest,
As foxes gather, feeling quite blessed.

Whispers of folly travel on air,
Chipmunks chortle without a care.
A badger who listens with eyes wide and round,
Snorts with laughter at the jokes he's found.

In the thicket, where shadows play games,
A raccoon crafts riddles with silly names.
Each chuckle ignites the moon's silver glow,
In this realm where giggles endlessly flow.

With every rustle, a punchline is born,
Nature's comedians delightfully adorn.
So gather close and share in the cheer,
For in this underbrush, joy hides near.

Jovial Journeys through Twisting Trails

On a path where the wildflowers sway,
Happiness blooms with each step of play.
A hedgehog rolls like a fuzzy ball,
As critters laugh, echoing the call.

Mice in costumes parade with a cheer,
While the butterflies dance, drawing near.
Tales take flight on the wind's gentle breath,
As laughter and beauty defy even death.

Through twisting trails of the forest's heart,
Every corner reveals a new part.
Bees buzz humor with nectar in hand,
Singing sweet songs of the grand woodland band.

With the sun as a spotlight shining bright,
The merry assembly takes off in flight.
For joys are found on each winding way,
In these jovial journeys that brighten the day.

Amusing Anecdotes of the Alder Grove

In the shade of alders, a story unfolds,
Where laughter is plated like treasures of gold.
A critter recounts of a vegetable heist,
While his friends giggle, excitement unpriced.

A parrot squawks tales of yesteryear,
With everyone listening, all lend an ear.
His vibrant plumage mirrors the fun,
As the crowd erupts when he's finally done.

A wise old owl nods at the chatter,
Sharing quips that only grandfathers flatter.
Every chuckle links them closer in glee,
In this animated gathering, wild and free.

As dusk falls gently upon the grove,
The stories continue, laughter to strove.
In the embrace of the branches' warm glove,
Amusing anecdotes of pure love.

Quips beneath the Quaking Aspens

In the grove where leaves can quiver,
Squirrels plot and schemers shiver.
A rabbit dons a hat quite tall,
While owls hoot and then they brawl.

Frogs croak jokes, quite absurd,
While fireflies glow with laughter heard.
A chipmunk slips, he takes a fall,
And beams a smile, not phased at all.

The breeze delights in playful schemes,
As shadows dance, all while it teems.
With every chirp and rustling leaf,
Laughter spreads beyond belief.

So join the fun, embrace the mirth,
In nature's jest, we find our worth.
Beneath the branches swaying spry,
The joy of jest will never die.

The Forest's Playful Murmurs

Within the pines, a riddle flows,
A badger cracks a joke, who knows?
A hedgehog snorts, oh what a sight,
As crickets chirp their song of light.

Squirrels see the tallest tree,
And challenge friends, come climb with me!
They tumble down, yet shout with glee,
For all the world's a comedy.

Beneath the boughs, the laughter soars,
As monkeys swing, they're never bored.
Each whisper hides a tale to tell,
Of friends who laugh and love so well.

In every nook, a chuckle's found,
With nature's jest, the heart's unbound.
So here we dwell, in jest and cheer,
The playful whispers draw us near.

Banter in the Bark

Beneath the oaks, a chatter swells,
As raccoons spin their playful tales.
A woodpecker taps with rhythm grand,
While turtles chuckle, slow and planned.

The ants discuss their grand parade,
While squirrels tease, not one dismayed.
Each crevice holds a quip or jest,
In nature's heart, we feel so blessed.

Through twisted roots and knotted twigs,
Laughter echoes, the joy it digs.
The fox sly grins, loves to mislead,
A brilliant ruse is all he needs.

So gather round, let banter fly,
The trees will laugh, the birds will sigh.
In this wild place of fun and cheer,
Our hearts will lighten, year by year.

Jocular Shadows and Starlit Silhouettes

When night descends, the fun begins,
The shadows dance, the laughter spins.
A raccoon dressed in outfits bright,
Steals the show in moonlit sight.

The owls hoot with gleeful sighs,
As fireflies paint the inky skies.
Each leafy branch, a frame for cheer,
As the woodlands whisper jokes so dear.

The echoes of the night resound,
With playful banter all around.
In the hush, a melody flows,
The mirth of nature brightly glows.

So as the stars begin to gleam,
Revel in this whimsical dream.
With jocular hearts, we roam tonight,
In nature's cheer, our spirits light.

Teasing Tunes of the Timberline

In the shade where shadows play,
Squirrels jest and lose their way.
Branches sway, a secret dance,
Nature laughs, give life a chance.

A chippy song floats on the breeze,
Talking trees shake off their leaves.
Nature's humor wrapped in green,
Giggles hide where eyes can't glean.

Dancing ferns and blooms that tease,
Join the fun, just as you please.
Echoes of laughter, soft and bright,
Fill the woods with pure delight.

The Laughing Leaves' Lullaby

Leaves that chuckle in the sun,
Tickling branches, oh what fun!
Rustling jokes that swirl and glide,
In this canopy, jokes can't hide.

Frolicking foxes play their part,
Telling tales that warm the heart.
A breeze that snickers, swirls around,
In these woods, a joy is found.

Berry bushes blush, they wink,
Nature's play, don't stop to think.
Each twig, each stone, a wisecrack stowed,
Amid the laughter, wisdom flowed.

Riddles Rooted in Rambling Trails

Hiking trails with jokes to share,
Every step pulls laughter near.
Roots that twist with playful glee,
Ask the stones what they can see.

Winding paths and echoes bright,
Surprises wait around each sight.
Leaves chuckle tales of what they've seen,
In this forest, fun's routine.

Every turn, a riddle spun,
Nature's humor has begun.
While the wild things laugh and tease,
Wander on and catch the breeze.

Gleeful Gabs from the Gnarled Giants

Old trees whisper, arms outstretched,
With secret stories, richly etched.
Gnarled roots and bark so wise,
Share their jokes in nature's guise.

In their shade, the critters come,
With playful bounces, laughs, and fun.
Ants parade, a marching band,
Joining in this joyful land.

Giant trunks with tales to tell,
Every crack, a giggle's spell.
Nature's jesters are here to stay,
In the wood's embrace, come laugh and play.

Pranks of the Ponderosa

The squirrel stole my sandwich, oh what a tease,
He giggled and darted, a master of sleaze.
A raccoon in the corner just rolled on the floor,
Laughing so hard, he could fetch me no more.

The pine cones are booming with secrets untold,
As gusts of wind whisper, 'Be daring, be bold!'
A fox with a wink just slipped on a log,
While a toad played the trumpet; the sound was a hog.

The beavers are scheming a water balloon,
A splash from the willow, oh what a boon!
With giggles and grins, they craft their parade,
In the shade they gather, a splash battle made.

So come take a peek at the pranks and the plays,
Amongst all the creatures in sunbeam's sweet rays.
With laughter and joy, all worries will cease,
In the heart of the forest, where mischief finds peace.

Cheeky Chatter among the Crickets

Crickets are chirping with playful delight,
Flipping through gossip, oh what a sight!
One's telling tales of a frog in the pond,
Who thinks he's a king with a crown and a wand.

The moonlight's a host for their party tonight,
Each chirp a punchline, each verse feels just right.
They mimic a cat with a swagger so proud,
While the fireflies flicker like stars in a crowd.

A cricket with sass sings a song so absurd,
About sneaking a snack from a peach that's disturbed.
With laughter contagious, they dance in a line,
In the chorus of chaos, their jokes intertwine.

So join in the revel, let spirits take flight,
With cheeky remarks that soar into the night.
In the symphony hidden, where laughter is free,
Chatter of crickets is pure harmony.

Mesmerizing Mirth in Mossy Nooks

In the nooks where the moss grows, laughter takes root,
A mushroom's a table, for games and a hoot.
The hedgehogs play poker with acorns and leaves,
While giggling through mischief, the owl just believes.

A sly little ferret spins tales in a whirl,
While the daisies whisper, they giggle and twirl.
The bees stop their buzzing—what's this? A new dance!
With honey-filled laughter, they leap at the chance.

The rabbits are rolling in soft, dewy grass,
Each tumble a fumble, just let courage pass.
With thumping and flumping, they leap in a daze,
Where mirth in the moss lifts the spirits ablaze.

So seek out the corners where smiles are in store,
In each mossy nook, there's a giggle galore.
With nature's own humor as backdrop, we bask,
In this whimsical world, no need for a mask.

Droll Dialogues of the Dappled Light

In the dappled light, where shadows play tricks,
A squirrel chats loudly, 'What's up with those sticks?'
The chipmunks all nod, they're quite in the know,
Laughing at branches that wave to and fro.

A wise old tortoise spills wisdom with style,
'Why hurry when laughter can stretch a good mile?'
With jokes like fine wine, they swirl in the sun,
Each quip shared among them, a festival of fun.

The butterflies flutter and join in the tease,
'Oh, did you hear what the snail said with ease?'
The shadows just giggle, the puddles all sigh,
As the sunbeams grumble, 'Oh, my! How they fly!'

So sit in the dappled, let conversations take flight,
In the spark of the moment, where humor feels right.
With each playful jest that dances on air,
The forest chuckles, a laughter we share.